Early Ontario Glass

by GERALD STEVENS

WHEN did glass-making begin?

Glass was the first material made by man.

Nature produces something similar, a black lava called obsidian from which Stone Age craftsmen fashioned tools and weapons. But man discovered for himself that silica sand, melted and left to set, forms a hard, impermeable substance with an infinite number of uses. The first crude attempts to produce glass seem to have been made more than 5000 years ago. Glass in the modern sense appeared about 1500 B.C., and since then the addition of soda, lime and other materials to the batch has resulted in improved varieties (see glossary, p. 15).

The first North American glass-house was established at Jamestown, Virginia, in 1608. More than two centuries passed, as far as we know, before the craft spread to Canada. There may have been a few small bootleg plants under French rule, but this seems unlikely because the authorities in Paris preferred to export such wares from the home market. After the conquest, the British held the same economic views: in 1763 George III issued an edict hostile to any new manufacturing in Canada.

It was left to an enterprising United Empire Loyalist, Nathaniel Mallory,

1

Covered sugar bowl—made in the first Canadian glass-house and now part of the ROM *Canadiana collections—is the most important single piece of early Canadian glass. Like all known products of the Mallorytown, Ontario, works it is free-blown of aquamarine coloured glass. The lily-pad decorations are superimposed, and the handles applied.*

to found the industry in this country. He had settled at Mallorytown Landing (named for the family), Leeds County, Ontario, in 1784, but soon moved a few miles north to establish the village of Mallorytown, midway between Brockville and Gananoque. There he began a cordwood business, a pack train for bringing supplies from Montreal and Kingston, a brickyard, and several other ventures. Among them, probably about 1825, was the first Canadian glass-house for which we have any evidence. It survived fitfully until the winter of 1839–40 when, according to an old newspaper report, it was closed "owing to the unreliableness of the foreman". No more was heard of it for many years except as a persistent but unproven local legend. Then in 1953 the writer discovered its former site, which was by that time a pasture, excavated the foundations, and eventually was able to identify several objects as having been manufactured there. The location is now listed as an Historic Site, and an official plaque has been placed in Mallorytown. Several Mallorytown pieces are in the Canadiana collections of the Royal Ontario Museum, where they are part of the finest public collection of early Canadian glass.

Following the Mallorytown venture, glass-making was attempted before Confederation in the Seigniory of Vaudreuil, Montreal, and St. Johns, in

Functional and sometimes beautiful, the common container was the staple product of Canada's early glass industry. It came in a variety of forms and colours: FROM THE LEFT, *pressed amber glass from Beaver Flint Glass Company, Toronto; mould-blown flint glass, Burlington Glass Works, Hamilton; pressed bottle glass, Hamilton Glass Works, Hamilton.*

Lower Canada, and at Hamilton in Upper Canada. The Montreal, St. Johns and Hamilton attempts were successful.

WHERE was glass made in Ontario?

The following is a check list of glass-houses operating in Ontario during the industry's first century:

MALLORYTOWN GLASS WORKS, Mallorytown (c. 1825–1839)

HAMILTON GLASS WORKS, Hamilton (1865–1895)

BURLINGTON GLASS WORKS, Hamilton (1875–1909)

NAPANEE GLASS WORKS, Napanee (1881–1883)

TORONTO GLASS WORKS, Toronto (1894–1900)

Why these locations?

The basic mixture in making glass is silicon, an alkali (usually soda or potash), lime, and cullet (glass from a previous melting). Other substances may be added in small quantities to produce special colours or qualities. These materials then must be heated to about 2200° F. in order to melt and combine.

In the early days of the Canadian industry, there were no economical means of carrying raw material long distances in bulk. The first consideration therefore in choosing the site of a nineteenth-century glass-house was silica sand—lots of it, close by. The second consideration was the availability of fuel: hardwood or, in the later part of the century, coal.

Invariably early Canadian glass-houses were located within three miles of large bodies of water. This brought them close to the U.S. border, but the infant industry was protected by tariffs against American competitors. Moreover, it was assured of a constant and recurring demand for containers, particularly for the preserving jars which were so important before the widespread use of tin cans. Without sealers, Ontario housewives would have had to depend largely on salted and dried foods throughout the winter months. Though these containers were its staple products, the industry served many other needs as well: just look about you and list the forms and types of glass within your range of vision!

How was glass manufactured?

The archaic glassmaker used a haphazard technique, which consisted of covering a specifically-shaped core with strips and gobs of molten glass until the required form was achieved. Then he scraped away the core and the object was complete.

The invention of the blowpipe changed all this. It gave mankind a tool of momentous importance, by which the craftsman gained full command of his medium. Now containers and decorative forms in shapes and sizes hitherto impossible could be produced in vast numbers.

A blowpipe is a hollow iron rod from three to six feet in length. One end, which is placed to the mouth, is tapered. The opposite end is flared. The

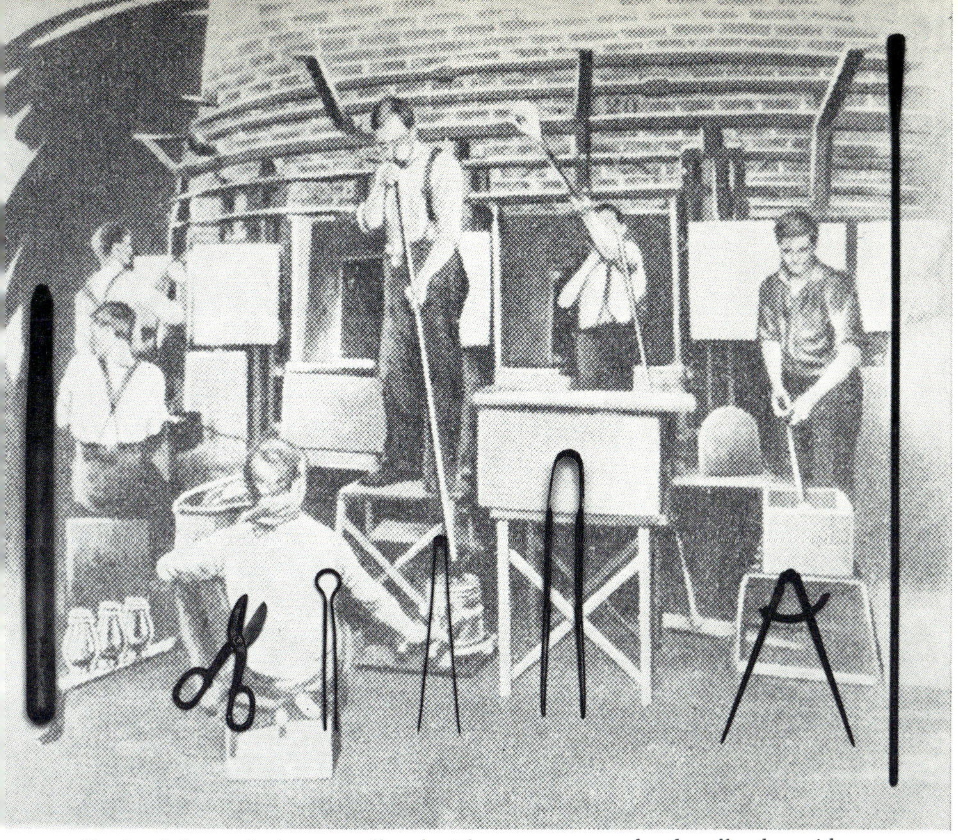

*Tools of the craft: iron pontil rod with screw-on wooden handle alongside;
shears; two spring tools; pucellas; compass; blowpipe. In the background scene,
typical of late 19th century plants, they are being used to make lamp chimneys.*

glass-blower dips the flared end into the molten batch and takes a gather,
which he then expands by blowing, and can shape and manipulate with the
following tools:

PONTIL (punty, puntee) ROD: a solid iron rod which he attaches to the base
of the object. This affords a handle with which to manipulate a glass object
having a heat of 1200° to 1500° F.

PUCELLAS: a U-shaped tool of a specific type made from iron.

SPRING TOOL: also U-shaped, but made to specifications supplied by indi-
vidual glass-blowers to the glass-house blacksmith. (A blacksmith was an
indispensable employee of every glassmaking establishment.)

SHEARS AND COMPASS (calipers): used to manipulate, shape and gauge
glass objects while in a plastic state.

BATTLEDORE: a paddle-shaped form of wood used to pat and smooth plastic
glass.

Many techniques have been used in the manufacture of glassware, and advanced technology is adding more. The basic ones include:

FREE-BLOWN (no moulds used): Any or all the basic tools may be used, but particularly the blowpipe and pontil rod. When the gather has been expanded, the pontil rod is attached and the blowpipe removed. The object is then shaped. Before it is placed in the lehr (the annealing oven), the pontil rod is broken free and the distinguishing characteristic of free-blown wares is revealed—a circular scar on the base. This scar could be removed with an abrasive wheel. Sometimes this did not suffice, and finer glass-cutting wheels were used; a polished circular depression provides evidence of this technique.

BLOWN MOULDED: In this process, a gather of glass was provided with a decorative design by use of a small, part-size mould. After being removed from the mould, while still on the blowpipe, the gather could be expanded, elongated, twisted and otherwise altered. The design, although contorted and diminished, remained constant. Blown moulded wares were finished by use of a pontil rod.

MOULD BLOWN (blown in a mould): This technique uses a mould the full size of the finished object. The wares may or may not show a pontil scar, but do exhibit seams or fins corresponding to the number of sections used in making the mould. Another distinguishing characteristic is an interior design that corresponds to that on the exterior—concave where the exterior is convex, and vice-versa.

PRESSED (hand operation): Nineteenth-century pressed glasswares were made in moulds operated by "pressmen." This was a manual operation and the result was sometimes quite crude. Moulds were made in two, three, four or more sections. Interiors of wares produced by this technique are smooth and do not follow exterior design.

MECHANICAL: The introduction of the machine sounded the death knell of the Canadian glass-blower. Automation was introduced about 1902 and in little more than a decade the automatic bottle blowing machine was installed in many Canadian firms. These machines were very complex, but provided uniformity of design and stepped-up production. One characteristic of containers produced in a wholly automatic glass-blowing machine is that the mould seams continue from base to lip and do not terminate below the lip as do those produced in a hand operation.

WHO were the glass-blowers?

The nineteenth-century glass-house allowed practice of personal skills and

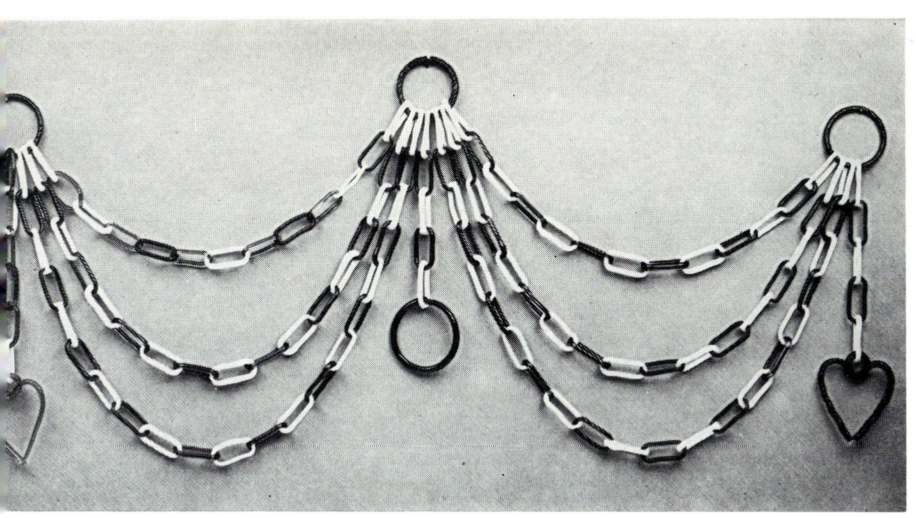

The glass "drape", a form of whimsey possibly unique to Canada, was highly desired by tavernkeepers who hung them on the walls instead of paintings. Whimseys were never sold for cash, but the glass-blowers and their host could usually reach an agreement which filled the tavern walls, to mutual satisfaction, with drapes, canes, hammers, hatchets, bells and swords of glass. Then a few weeks would pass . . . and somehow, one Saturday night a donnybrook would break out, fragmenting scores of collectors' items but opening the way to new arrangements. This example is a rare tricoloured drape of amber, opal and blue links, made at the Sydenham (Dominion) Glass Company in Wallaceburg.

a freedom of movement that is lacking in the present period of automation. If a glass-house suffered a breakdown, rival establishments vied for its qualified glass-blowers, who were enticed to Toronto, Wallaceburg, Montreal and the Maritimes. American glass-houses offered special pay and costs of transportation.

Glass-blowers were known as the aristocracy of labour, but they earned their pay, which was high, under almost insufferable conditions—continual heat up to and above 100°. Many nineteenth-century glass-houses ceased operations entirely during July and August. When he wasn't working, the old-time glass-blower was apt to be playing—at horse races, baseball games, cock fighting—or rinsing away the heat and fumes of the glass-houses.

Tall tales are told by the few survivors. In the historic city of Hamilton, legends live on of glass-blowers parading on Labour Day wearing glass hats, carrying glass swords, glass knives, and glass pistols, and brandishing glass canes at bystanders. What a sight that must have been—and what a loss of collectors' items!

WHAT did each house make?

MALLORYTOWN: Ontario's first glass-house produced free-blown, aquamarine coloured sugar bowls and covers, pitchers, flasks, milk bowls, doorstops and many types of containers. The batch materials were obtained locally, and consisted of silica sand, wood-ash potash, and lime. The aquamarine colour, typical of all authenticated specimens, was caused by iron oxides in the Potsdam sandstone.

Another rare Mallorytown product of aquamarine coloured glass, free-blown, with threaded neck, applied handle and superimposed lily-pad decoration. The author obtained this footed pitcher at a country auction, where it was knocked down at the first low bid because a crack made it "valueless".

HAMILTON GLASS WORKS: The firm was established in Hamilton in 1865 by Gatchell, Moore & Co., but eight years later George Rutherford & Co. became proprietors. The staff included many notable glass-blowers, among them the Bard family (Andrew, George A. and Thomas), Joseph Charlton, W. B. Griner and G. E. Harris.

Although accurate lists of dates and employees have been compiled, the products remain somewhat of a mystery. We know that it manufactured green and amber bottle glass, and advertised its willingness to make "private moulds of every description." Research suggests that it produced containers but did not attempt the more complicated forms of tableware. Authenticated specimens include commercial bottles, preserve jars and other types of containers, and whimseys in the form of canes, hats, door-stops, witch balls, etc.

The Hamilton works was long remembered for a spectacular collapse of

Special chemicals added to the batch produced a translucent product known as opal glass. This set of pressed milk-white creamer, covered sugar and spooner was made at the Burlington Glass Works, Hamilton.

its tank furnace. The molten batch flowed out of the glass-house and across the street "just like Vesuvius" according to elderly residents who told me "the lava took hours to cool".

BURLINGTON GLASS WORKS: This was the most prolific Canadian glass-house of its day. Its production exceeded that of any other firm, included every form and colour of glass, and made use of every technique then known.

The plant stood on the eastern limits of the city of Hamilton: the name refers to Burlington Bay, *not* to the nearby town of Burlington with which the company had no connection. The first printed reference to it appears to be in the Hamilton city directory of 1875. The proprietors then were

Glass paperweights, often with gaily coloured decorations inside, were fashioned in spare moments as presentation pieces. This "Billy McGinnis" type, with a five-petalled lily in the centre, was made at the Burlington Glass Works for a Mr. Hunt.

E. R. Kent & Co., but the directory of 1878–79 lists M. A. Kerr and W. G. Beach, and the following year W. G. Beach alone is mentioned as manager.

Techniques employed by the Burlington glass-blowers included free-blown, blown-moulded, blown in a mould, and pressed. Types of glass produced were opal, blue opal, custard, flint (clear), red, blue, amber, green, and various shades thereof. Glasswares included bottles, sealers (preserve jars), lamps, lamp chimneys, salts and tablewares.

Among the colourful glass-blowers employed in the Burlington works were three of "gaffer" and "finisher" qualifications who contributed specific techniques to Canadian glass-making. William "Billy" McGinnis is remembered by a type of five-petalled lily paperweight which bears his name. George Mullin's name is given to another style of paperweight, of flint glass encasing mushroom-like groups of coloured glass chips. The third innovator, Patrick "Pat" Wickham, inspired his co-workers to make aquamarine-coloured bottle glass paperweights containing a rectangular strip of opal glass on which was written the name of the person for whom the weight was made. Examples of paperweights made by all three men are included in the Edith Chown Pierce-Gerald Stevens collection of early Canadian glass in the Sigmund Samuel Canadiana Building of the ROM.

NAPANEE GLASS WORKS: This firm had a short, unhappy life, and today is remembered principally for a specific type of mercury glass candlestick. Its founder, John Herring, was a classic example of the energetic man who extends his interests beyond his own knowledge. An American immigrant,

10

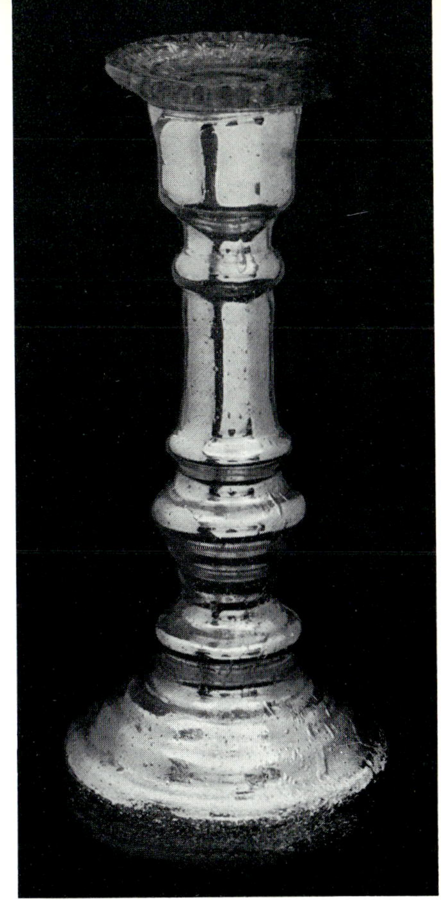

Herring settled in Napanee in the 1840s and established himself in manufacturing, brickmaking, lumbering and construction. In 1881 he branched out into the production of window glass, a field of which he knew nothing. Though craftsmen were imported from Germany and the United States, the venture failed, and in a final desperate attempt to recoup his losses Herring turned to glasswares which were not mass-produced but made to order, among them globes for street lights and druggists' wares. In 1883, he was forced to close.

TORONTO GLASS COMPANY: Established in 1894, this company was absorbed by rival interests in 1900. It was a "container" plant, with a commercial production limited to bottles, preserve jars, etc. The personnel included many well-known Canadian glass-blowers, among them John and Tom McNichol, John C. and James F. Malcolmson, and Patrick Wickham.

SYDENHAM GLASS WORKS: In 1891 an English Great Lakes captain, J. W. Taylor, saw large deposits of sand along the shore near Wallaceburg—and conceived the idea of a glass factory. The first attempt was a failure, but in

1894 the first batch of glass was achieved. Since then the plant at Wallaceburg has always given particular attention to glasswares. It still produces many types of tableware as part of Dominion Glass Company Limited, in which it and several other glass-houses were combined in 1913.

This house has played an important part in the history of the Canadian industry. It was here that glass-blowers flocked when earlier nineteenth-century firms closed their doors. In addition to commercial glass they produced a great variety of whimseys including canes, birds, hats, bells, hammers and hatchets. And here, too, many French-Canadian craftsmen were moved after a breakdown, early in this century, at the old Delormier Street plant of the Diamond Flint Glass Company in Montreal. The co-mingling of varied approaches to glass-blowing, especially in whimseys, produced many forms unique in Canada.

BEAVER FLINT GLASS COMPANY: This was one of the few Canadian glass-houses to operate under its original name for more than 50 years. The Beaver works in Toronto were "Manufacturers and Importers of Druggists', Chemists' and Scientific Glassware." The "Beaver" preserve jar also is credited to this firm, but experts now believe it was made for them by the old Sydenham plant at Wallaceburg. Indeed, there now is proof that

12

Maple leafs were long a popular decorative motif on Canadian glass. Pressed flint glass salver comes from the Jefferson Glass Company of Toronto.

Dominion Glass Company Limited produced several moulds for Beaver Flint Glass.

JEFFERSON GLASS COMPANY: The U.S.-owned Jefferson Glass Company opened a subsidiary in Toronto in 1913, but within months, in the general amalgamation of Canadian glass-houses, the plant was acquired by Dominion Glass Company Limited. As that company's Jefferson works, it played an important part in the epic of Canadian glass. Although founded in the twentieth century, it continued production of glasswares designed in the closing decades of the nineteenth century and until 1925 manufactured many forms of glass which are treasured today as collectors' items—thus enriching our heritage in a medium which is delicate, and all too rare in surviving examples.

13

Two other popular designs in pressed flint glass from the Jefferson Glass Company. ABOVE, *Beaded Oval and Fan. No. 2 (No. 230 ware) nappy and tall celery dish.* BELOW, *Daisy and X Band (No. 240 ware) half-gallon jug and miniature set.*

Annealing: the gradual cooling or tempering of hot glasswares in the lehr (leer); initial temperature 950° F.

Batch: raw materials ready for melting in a pot, tank or other type of furnace; melted ingredients ready for blowing, pressing, etc. Temperature for melting 2200° F.

Bottle glass: basic glass composed of silica sand, soda, and lime; colours vary from pale green and aquamarine through dark amber.

Container: bottles of every type; preserve jars (sealers), etc.

Crystal: correctly, lead glass: used by manufacturers to describe any clear, colourless glass.

Cullet: glass saved from a previous melting. A percentage of cullet is added to every new batch.

Dip mould: One-piece mould.

Finisher: a master craftsman; one who removes mould marks from upper sections of goblets, bowls, etc. Finished glass sold for a higher price.

Free-blown glass: glasswares finished without the aid of moulds.

Frit: partially cooked and fused ingredients saved and added to a batch.

Full-size mould: sectional mould approximately the size of finished glasswares.

Gaffer: master glass-blower; head of a "shop" or group of men. Shops varied in numbers according to type of glasswares being produced.

Gather: molten glass removed from the batch at the gathering end of a blowpipe.

Glassmakers' soap: oxide of manganese. When correct proportions of this "soap" are added to the batch, the natural colour (bottle glass) is neutralized. Incorrect proportions result in an eventual change of colour.

Glory Hole (late): small movable furnace used for reheating, finishing and fire polishing.

Green Glass: see Bottle glass.

Lead Glass: metal made with oxide of lead as a flux. True "cut" and "crystal" glass. Characteristics—weight and resonance.

Lehr (leer): oven for tempering or annealing finished glasswares. Temperature constants for working glass:

Glass Furnace, between pots 2507° F.	In the pots, working .... 1913° F.
In the pots, refining .... 2390° F.	Annealing .... 950° F.

Lime Glass: glass made with soda and lime as a flux according to a formula discovered in 1864 and resulting in a clear non-lead glass of some brilliance but little resonance.

Marver: polished metal or stone slab on which the gather of glass is rolled.

Metal: glassmaker's term for glass in a molten or finished state.

Parison: initial inflation of a gather of glass.

Part-size Mould: a small mould with an interior design used in making blown-moulded glasswares.

Piece Mould: used in manufacturing mould-blown or pressed glasswares.

Pontil (punty, puntee) Rod: see text, page 5.

Pontil Mark: see text, page 6.

Pressed Glass: see text, page 6.

Pucellas: see text, page 5.

Spring Tool: see text, page 5.

Taker-in (carrying-in boy): apprentice who carries finished glasswares to lehr.

Welded Rim: little used term. English, American, and Canadian writers use "folded rim." When applied to a foot or rim this term indicates that such areas are finished by in- or out-folding the edge of blown glasswares.

Whimsey: a non-commercial glass object produced to demonstrate a glass-blower's personal command of the medium—presentation paperweights, hats, canes, birds, drapes, etc.